To water babies everywhere.

By ....
and the Millinson Family

My Mummy has got a
baby in her tummy.
It is in a special place called a uterus.
The uterus is like a stretchy bag which
holds the baby tight like a cuddle.

Having a baby sometimes means
that Mummy feels tired
and sometimes she is sick.

You can't see the baby
because it is inside Mummy
but as the baby gets bigger
Mummy's tummy gets bigger too.

It takes nine months for the baby
to be ready to be born.
That is a long time.

I like to cuddle mummy's tummy. I can feel our baby wriggling and kicking. We call our baby

....

.... might be a boy or might be a girl.

Sometimes we feel Mummy's tummy
and try to guess which part of our
baby we can feel.
It could be an arm, a leg
or even a bottom!

While our baby is inside Mummy's
tummy a special tube carries all the
things that the baby needs to grow.
It is joined to Mummy at one end
and to the baby's tummy at the other.

Once the baby has been born
he doesn't need the tube any more.
Mummy will be able to feed
the baby milk from her boobs.

Mummy is having our baby at home.

When the baby is being born the midwife stays with us and helps Mummy and the baby. It can take a long time for a baby to be born.

The special stretchy bag helps to squeeze the baby through a special hole near Mummy's bottom. Muscles that keep the baby in slowly open and let the baby out.

We had a big pool of water. Mummy sat in it. I said, "That bath's got no taps." We filled it using a hose pipe. We all got in. I put my boats in it. Later, the water helped the baby to come out. We had all the things that baby needs like a towel and some clothes.

When our baby was born
we were all very happy.
we called them

. . . .

The story continued.
Four years late Ben made a splash
like his brother Joe.

Paulette and Sally, two wonderful
midwives helped us birth him.

Sally Stockley died in 2003
We remember her with love and
gratitude.

About the editor:

Shona Kitchener, Director of Barefoot Birth Pools Ltd. first met Kirsten at Peterborough Homebirth Group shortly before the birth of her second child. Shona instantly fell in love with the home made book Kirsten had brought along and asked if Kirsten would be happy for her to produce a new version which could be made available for more families to enjoy. Two years, and two babies later That Bath's Got No Tap's is now available internationally on Amazon, and exclusively through Shona's business Barefoot Birth Pools.

About Barefoot Birth Pools:

Barefoot Birth Pools support families with the planning of their home water birth by providing birth pool and related equipment hire along with other waterbirth accessories. Caring deeply about the experience of every family they work with Barefoot Birth Pools have provided the highest level of customer service to over three thousand customers in the last seven years. To continue to promote and encourage home waterbirths around the country Barefoot Birth Pools also offer Community Birth Pool Schemes to support hospitals setting up home birth teams and Waterbirth Workshops for midwives and birth professionals.

www.BarefootBirthPools.co.uk